QUEST FOR RESPECT

By

Linda Braswell

Pathfinder Publishing
of California
Ventura, CA

QUEST FOR RESPECT

A Guide To Healing For Survivors of Rape

Edited By: Eugene D. Wheeler

Published By:

PathfinderPublishing of California
458 Dorothy Avenue
Ventura, CA 93003
(805) 642-9278

Second Printing 1990
Second Edition, 1992
Third Printing 1992
Fourth Printing 1995
Fifth Printing, 1996

Library of Congress Cataloging-in-Publication Data

Braswell, Linda, 1941-
Quest for Respect: A guide to healing for survivors of rape
    p.   cm.
    Bibliography: p.
    Includes index.
    1. Rape victims — Mental health. 2. Self-respect. I. Title
    RC560.R36B73 1989
    362.88'3 — dc20 89-9274
    CIP
ISBN 0-934793-44-1

DEDICATION

For My Daughter

CYNTHIA HARRIS

ACKNOWLEDGMENTS

This book gives voice to the rape survivors I have served. They taught me how to help. They shared their stories, their pain and their successes which made this book possible. I am grateful to them. It is with humility that I offer first their stories and my learning from them on how to help heal.

My colleagues, Deborah Caddy, Carolyn Cantrell, Brenda-Coldeway, Linda Fredrikson, Donna Herber, Grace Lehmann, Susan Loving-Harris and Kelly Spencer read the manuscript, offered their experience, encouraged and supported my effort.

Janice Harris Lord, author of *No Time For Goodbyes* and *Beyond Sympathy* demonstrated her faith in me by introducing me to my publisher, Eugene Wheeler. Both offered valuable suggestions and gentle encouragement when needed.

A very special thank you to Stacey Stover who kept me on schedule and typed many drafts. Shari Shanafelt, Director for Victim Assistance offered advice on the criminal justice process section and typed the final draft. The dedication and organizational skill of these two women contributed enormously to the effort.

My husband, David Sullivan, devoted hours to the care of the author by listening, supporting and encouraging me. He believed in me. He reassured me that I had something valuable to offer and consistently discouraged self-doubt.

I also thank Eugenie Wheeler for her editing contributions and Josh Young for his cover design.

And so, I offer *Quest For Respect* to survivors of the crime of rape in the belief that healing is possible. Above all, I have great respect for the victims who pick up the pieces of their lives and become stronger, wiser and embrace new life with faith and courage.

Linda Braswell

April, 1992

FOREWORD

Rape is an ancient crime. All over the world, the cruelty of sexual abuse has raged generation after generation for thousands and thousands of years. But Longevity doesn't make it right. Or inevitable.

Modern anthropologists have identified a few existing cultures where there is no sexual abuse. Their common ingredient seems to be respect—for self, for others, for nature—and an ethos of partnership rather than domination. Rape prone cultures such as ours, on the other hand, are marked by predatory violence encouraged by an ideal of domination.

Whenever he is culturally positioned as lord over nature, "man" (not the generic term!) inherits an old and basic permission to be dominant and therefore arrogant, persistant, and even violent in pursuit of power. In this environment, unless checked by a gentle nature or other more tolerant ideals, individual and group life likely becomes a competition for power, mostly among men, with daily winners and losers.

Victims of this pervasive, exploitive world view are generally women and children, gentle men, all people ethnically and culturally different from the power elite, and the natural world, with all its gifts and creatures. Notice that this is a long list.

The primary means of dominance and control have been wrong naming ("these people are genetically inferior"), economic slavery and exploitation ("being inferior, you deserve less"), fear and threats ("don't rock the boat or you'll really suffer"), and violence, including the rape of cultures we call war, the rape and destruction of human beings, and the methodical rape—as opposed to respectful use—of the natural world. Notice that these are effective strategies, impossible to defeat without a dramatic shift in human consciousness.

Today this kind of shift seems to be in progress. We can feel its emergence even in this period of great worldwide destruction and violence. Its signs are evident in a persistant and growing criticism of the brutal ways of habitual dominance and power, in a questioning of old values, assumptions, and paradigms, and in the challenging voices of the modern movements on behalf of women, civil rights, children's safety, peace, nuclear disarmament, and conservation of the environment.

This book, written to help you recover from sexual assault and abuse, is part of that big shift in human consciousness. Though small and gentle in its conversational tone, it vigorously exposes the old "rape myths" for what they are—lies, added insults, ugly propaganda of the old, destructive ethos of violence.

This little book's primary messages are that healing is possible and that healing is triumphant. When you heal and when you move on courageously with life, the rapist hasn't won. You have won.

The intention of the author of this book is to help you heal and to help you win. She and I and all our colleagues everywhere want for you not just healing, but victory over pain and fear and tragedy.

Whoever you are, as you walk toward recovery, remember that other women, men, and children have a stake in your triumph—other survivors of violence, committed and compassionate advocates, and believers in new visions and new human possibilities.

Thoughts of them and the tools in this book comfort, energize, and sustain you as you move toward healing and triumph.

Karen Perkins, Executive Director
The Women's Center of Tarrant County
Fort Worth, Texas

CONTENTS

INTRODUCTION

While leading a group for rape survivors, a young woman named Ashli asked for something to read to help her healing process. That was the genesis of this book. Moreover, I became acutely aware of the need of survivors who didn't have access to trained people during my telephone conversations (call-ins) on *COPE*, a TV call-in show produced by the ACTS Cable network. In both urban and rural areas, survivors suffer alone. In isolation, they believe that the rape was their fault and they live with guilt and despair.

This book was written to do two things: to educate rape survivors, to help them know that rape is a crime, that it is never the victim's fault, and to guide them, to help them restore their personal power, and heal their hearts and spirits. I hope it will be used as a partner on this pilgrimage. I hope its pages will be well worn at journey's end. I know it will help.

Five main tasks need to be accomplished, hence five chapters. The first is to acknowledge the impact on your life, to name how the rape has changed your life. The second task is to make a commitment to yourself to heal and to gather your resources around you. The third asks you to relive the rape through the telling of your story. Because it hurts, without the commitment you make in Chapter Two, the pain of reliving it becomes too great. So take your time and fortify yourself well in Chapter Two. Chapter Four turns toward the future. It asks that you make new decisions about the relationships you want in your life, while Chapter Five asks that you let the pain go. The last step is necessary for the wounds to heal in a healthy way.

Since the crime of rape is mostly acted out by men, the book uses the male pronoun. Society, in general, has been even less willing to believe men who have been raped and has been generally unsupportive. It happens to men by other men and some men have been raped by women. It is hoped that male survivors will feel as supported as women while reading this book.

As stated throughout the book, the healing is yours. It must be done by you, with respect for your survivorship. It must be done in your own time.

ONE

THE IMPACT OF RAPE

Life is like an onion you peel it off one layer at a time, and sometimes you weep.

Carl Sandberg

You are hurting. You are angry or depressed. Your life is caving in around you and your relationships are not the same as before the rape. Perhaps you can't get close to those you love the most, like you used to do. Maybe you feel that you're not a good person anymore. Perhaps you believe that everyone who sees you knows that you were raped. The worst thing though, is that you think you may be crazy because the rape happened a few weeks ago, maybe a couple of months or even years ago. And you think you should be "over it" by now.

The first thing to understand is that these feelings are normal. When you experience a rape, your thoughts are on how to survive. No one consents to rape. No one willingly cooperates with a rapist. And yet, to survive, you must submit to save your own life. Because you were smart, because you knew that surviving was the most important thing, you may have cooperated with the demands of the person who raped you. And the feeling that remains with you is guilt. You feel guilty that you didn't fight or struggle more. You feel badly because maybe you were "looking too good." You attracted the rapist. You think that if you had not gone to the store alone, or so late at night...or if you had locked your window, this would not have happened.

Maybe the person who raped you was someone you knew. The rapist was someone you were dating, met at a party or was your own partner. What that experience brings to mind is "Why didn't I see this coming?" "What is wrong with my judgement that I made such a poor decision?" "How could I let this happen to me—I'm so ashamed." What follows self blame then is you begin to make yourself accountable for the action of another. You take into yourself the responsibility for the rape which leads to feelings of shame and guilt.

Finally, you feel numb, scared, angry, depressed, guilty, ashamed, dirty, not hungry, and unable to sleep. When this happens it's time to talk about it, to understand it, and to take your PERSONAL POWER back. It's time to reclaim your life to build it back the way you want it to be. It's time to love and laugh again, to feel joy, to feel confident, and to feel close to friends again.

You will not forget what happened. Your rage will never completely go away. It takes courage to heal—to look at what happened, and to relive it in the telling of the experience. By reading this book, you are considering a new beginning and starting to reclaim your life. This is an important step. Congratulate yourself! You CAN heal. You CAN put the rape in perspective so that this experience does not have power over you. If you're ready, let's begin. And remember, you don't have to go through it alone.

Was It My Fault?

What happened to you was not an accident. People who rape do so because they choose to. No one forces them. No one holds their loved ones hostage or threatens their life, as perhaps someone did to you. The use of force and power incites rapists. They may fantasize about what it would be like to "take you" against your will. To rape is their choice. They alone are responsible for their bad behavior and for their crime.

Rape happens to thousands of others every year. Rape happens once every six minutes in the United States. Accurate figures are impossible to obtain because the majority of rapes go unreported. The FBI estimates that only one in ten are reported to authorities. "In the United States," says Surgeon General C. Everett Koop, "as many as 15 million women have been beaten, raped or suffered other forms of physical and sexual assault, with the number rising by 1 million a year." (Ft. Worth Star Telegram. March 10, 1989.)

You are not alone.

WHY ME?

Many survivors' first questions are, "Why did he rape me? What did I do to attract his attention? What did I do to deserve this? Why didn't he choose someone else?"

These questions are an attempt to make sense out of an event which is in itself senseless. You may think that if you can make sense out of the rape, you will gain some understanding of what happened and learn from the tragedy. Perhaps you believe that if you change your future behavior you will be safe. You'll be in control. Maybe you say to yourself that the rape happened because you wore a certain dress or shorts or a perfume that attracted him, or because you were in a place you shouldn't have been. If you can make sense out of the rape the same mistake will be avoided and you will be safe.

Some people believe that if something bad happens to us it is because we did something to deserve it. They think that the world is a just place, and if you do what's expected of you then good things in life will happen to you. And if you do the "right" things, no harm will come to you.

But, the truth is that you had nothing to do with the rape. You are not special in that way. Rape is a crime mostly of opportunity, the person who raped you knows that. The rapist probably planned to rape and looked for a chance and a victim. In fact, most rapists take the time to know the victims and to gain their confidence. They do that because it makes it easier to commit the crime.

Rape has little to do with sex. Does it surprise you that most rapists have normal sexual outlets? Sex is a weapon a rapist uses to degrade and humiliate victims in order to feel powerful and masterful over another person. Major myths in our society are that women ask to be raped, that "she got what she deserved" and that "only gay men get raped." For centuries rapists have been excused by society. The victim is supposedly to blame because many believe that the woman was responsible for the rape no matter how violent or deviant. They might say, "It is just sex that got out of control." Another commonly held belief is that women have no right to express their sexuality in dress or behavior without "coming across" on demand.

Because rape is unique, the only crime in which personal boundaries are so clearly invaded, the strategies victims use with other crimes are inadequate to cope with the crisis of rape. Survivors may try to focus on the cause of the sexual assault thinking this will help them to cope with the crises. What you need to do to recover is to move past reason, to give up prospects that you can make sense of it. Rape doesn't make sense. Rape is inhumane—Rape IS a "four letter word."

So how do you recover from the fear, anxiety, guilt, shame, depression, anger and the other emotions that result from this assault? It is a crime that brings into question your sense of self, your sense of control over your environment and your ability to solve problems. The first step in this process is to acknowledge and identify how the assault has affected your life. And it does affect your life in many ways.

There is no such thing as a "typical rape" or a "typical rape survivor." Your reactions are unique to you as an individual. However you react to a rape is normal. In every case, what you

6

did to survive is the right thing to have done. It was not your fault. What is important to remember is that rape is fundamentally an act of violence. Rape is a total violation of your rights over your own body and of your ability to make a choice. From a woman's point of view, the sexual dimension of rape is usually less important than the violent aspects. For men, their sexuality is sometimes called into question. "Does this mean I'm gay? What about me attracted him to me?" It is important to know that the motivation of the rapist remains the same (power and control) whether the victim is a man or woman.

Nearly all rapes involve threats of bodily harm, and in some cases the survivors do suffer physical injury. It is important to remember that what you reacted to was the threat that you, or someone you love, would be hurt if you didn't cooperate. If you submitted to the rapist's demands, you may feel that you somehow consented. Consider that your submission was a survival strategy. Rape, by definition, does not give one a choice. So whatever the circumstances of your rape, it was not your fault because you had no real choice.

Why Do I Feel Guilty?

Many survivors have some degree of self-blame. Thoughts like "If I hadn't let him spend so much money on me," or "I invited him in, after all," demonstrates that many survivors believe they share in the blame. Survivors may also feel guilty because they couldn't stop the assault. Many survivors say, "I couldn't believe this was really happening and that I could do nothing to stop it." But guilt can be used to help a person gain control. For instance, if statements like the above have occurred to you, then you can tell yourself that from now on you will pay your own way and not invite dates in. That way you can be assured that rape won't happen to you again.

Probably the most common reason for guilt is that survivors are forced to participate in their own dehumanization. Survivors are more afraid of what will happen if they don't submit than what will happen if they do. Therefore, many survivors comply with the rapists' demands. Survivors sense intuitively that if they don't cooperate, they could be hurt more and perhaps not survive.

Reactions to Rape

The single most terrifying reaction to being raped is the fear of being killed or mutilated. The rapist doesn't have to actually make the threat aloud or show a weapon for a person to feel danger. As one woman put it, "I figured if he was crazy enough to do this to me, he was crazy enough to kill me." Each woman reading that sentence probably understands her thoughts at a level that is at the very core of her being. Survivors respond to the rape depending on several factors—the most important being the kind of person they are.

As mentioned above, the fear of being killed or maimed is foremost on a survivor's mind during the actual assault, and will dictate how she reacts. For instance, if you are awakened out of a deep sleep, the shock of finding someone in your bed usually produces a stunned reaction. But if the attack is not so sudden, survivors often remember every detail of the assault and plan how to escape when it's over.

When confronted with the unexpectedness of an assault of any kind, there are three possible choices: You can fight, try to escape, or freeze. Most survivors automatically, without thinking, choose the one that will work for them to save their lives. Another fairly common response is to feel a complete separation of mind and body. It's as if the rape were happening to someone else.

In the end, recovery depends on who you are, how you handle stress in general, the amount of violence, the length of time the attack went on, and whether or not you knew the attacker. Later chapters will suggest a guide for your recovery.

Immediately after the rape, the usual reaction is shock. It is hard to believe—it's like a cruel nightmare. One woman bit herself on the arm to make sure she was still alive. Others are stunned and wander about in a daze. These reactions are normal to the most traumatic event in one's life and are similar to the ones people have who go through any other terrible crisis such as a war, flood or tornado. They are common reactions to an awful ordeal which produces terror and shock.

Some survivors may act calm, sensible or even indifferent. They may smile in a tense way, crack jokes or act in a casual way about what happened. This kind of behavior is the way people protect themselves from shock, and it is a way for them to cope at first with an unbelievable event.

Fear and Anxiety

During the first phase of healing, which lasts about a month, rape leaves the survivor emotionally disorganized. The survivor finds it difficult to make decisions. It is hard to know how to plan for the next moment, not to mention the rest of your life. If the rape happened outside, then you are afraid to be outside. If the rape happened inside, you are afraid to be inside. Since most of us live our lives inside and outside, the results of rape from the beginning restrict where you can be comfortably. Survivors are afraid to be alone and yet crowds make them nervous. The overriding emotion is fear.

Simple decisions are agony. Anxiety is a constant companion. Sounds in the work place or at home that were never noticed before, become threats that must be examined. For example, survivors may awake startled to the sound of a heater turning on, or the normal creaks of the house. The sound of a door opening or a window being raised become reasons for alarm. The usual, common place sounds and sights in the environment demand attention. You have no choice in your reactions. Everything has meaning and everything feels like a threat that must be investigated. The fear can leave you raw and on the alert 24 hours a day.

Nightmares

Sleep becomes elusive. There seems to be no way to rest because of the hyper-vigilance. If you are able to fall asleep, it is only a light sleep that can be interrupted by the smallest sound. Rest is needed yet there seems to be no way to get it. And when you sleep, nightmares of the rape may be replayed night after night. You may arise exhausted only to face a day filled with thoughts that won't stop. Thoughts that can't be diverted, repressed or turned off, haunt your waking hours. It's like a tune that you can't get out of your mind, except that this is a nightmare that you relive again and again.

Shame

Rape humiliates. The most precious and private parts of your body have been violated. Against your will you've been forced to participate in that degradation. You may feel dirty in a way that soap and water will not take away. Many survivors bathe repeatedly, trying the only way they know to cleanse themselves. When it doesn't work, the anger rises because you feel powerless to help yourself. Then, because as human beings, powerlessness feels like failure, it gets turned inward, twisted in a strange way and translated into guilt.

For most people the most intimate way to express love to another is through sexuality, and that way has been compromised. You may not feel free to accept intimate touching, and because you have been invaded and can't get out of yourself, you may not be able to give touching either. Those people in your life who are there for you, who offer comfort and love must wait, and you must wait. It's like one more avenue for closeness is denied. You are trapped in your body and in your mind with no way to escape.

You may search for new ways to cope with what has happened. You may say to yourself and others, "I'm fine. It happened and now I just want to get on with my life. I want to put it behind me, and I don't want to talk about it anymore." This decision is necessary because you cannot go on living with uncontrolled fear and anxiety. When your usual ways of coping with disaster are destroyed, as they often are with rape, it is natural to develop new ones. It is usually the only course open and you may take it with determination. You decide to follow the only way out and make heroic efforts to forget what happened.

Must Go On

The second phase looks and feels as if you are making a good adjustment. You go back to work, you resume your life as lover, parent and partner. You try to connect again with people and things that held importance to you before the rape. You try to get back to "normal". Typically, however, things begin to go wrong. Your self confidence begins to lag. Things that you felt positive about before come into question. You become unsure of yourself. For example, after her rape, a young accountant began to doubt her ability to do her job. She had been quite successful and was advancing in her profession. Because she was an auditor, her job required her to travel and stay in unfamiliar hotels. Her rape had occurred at night in her apartment and sleep was elusive. Spending night after night in different beds, unable to rest, she began to distrust her ability to do the work for which she was so well trained. Her confidence began to slip.

Depression/Anger

Your energy level begins to drop and you feel tired and want to sleep. A kind of irritability sets in. It shows up in your relationships with other people important in your life. You may have an unexplained short fuse that complicates your work and home life. Patience and generosity of spirit evaporate and you snap at co-workers, partners, parents, or children. Your ability to trust anyone or anything begins to vanish, and anger lurks just below the surface. When those around you begin to confront you on your behavior, you are apt to lack any explanation, and because you can't explain it, the dark cloud of depression grows.

Because the struggle to put the rape behind you is successful, you don't relate the rape to the changes in your behavior. The reason for the feelings and behavior is the rape, but it's hard to understand. With great resolve you push the memory of the rape down below the surface because you can't live with that constant fear and anxiety. On the other hand, it is destroying the quality of your life. It's coming back in a form that you don't recognize and it is impacting your life in an uncontrollable way.

Some of your precious relationships may degenerate, yet you may feel powerless to stop it. You might blame yourself because after all, it is you who have changed. This is the point at which you are likely to seek help. But because the rape is something you are trying hard to forget, you probably don't tell your friends, relatives, or counselors about it, and the help or advice they offer does little good.

Suicide

As the choices seemingly diminish, and hurt, pain and confusion increase, the idea of suicide can occur. Most survivors don't want to die. Most survivors just want life to be like it was before the rape. But with the knowledge that it is not possible to go back and the road ahead seems obliterated, suicide for a few becomes an option. The tragedy when death by suicide occurs is immeasurable to families and friends. The hopes and dreams are forever gone and in some ironic way—the rapist wins! If you find yourself feeling that you have no other options stop now and call a suicide hotline. As one woman wrote, "I am not alone . . . maybe there is a way to get through the darkness without having to put an end to my physical life." Under no circumstances is it fair to give the rapist any power. Call now.

Rape Has Changed My Life

It takes as much courage to embrace the hurt of the rape as it takes to survive it. It is necessary. It is the only way out of the darkness that has enveloped your life.

STEPS TO TAKE

Begin now to evaluate the ways in which this assault has affected your life.

Questions to ask yourself:

- Do you doubt your own abilities? In what ways?
- Are your relationships as warm and open as you want them to be? If not, how have they changed?
- Are you as good a partner, parent, student, lover, worker as you were before? If not, how are you different?

Action To Take:

- List the ways your life has changed since the rape.

If you find that you have changed in ways that are not working for you, it is NOT your fault. You are not a bad or incompetent person. The rape has caused the problems. It is your job now to take an inventory of what's wrong and to make the commitment to yourself to feel the pain of healing. This is the first step. When you are ready, move ahead. Chapter Two is about preparing to do the work. And, remember, you don't have to do it alone.

NOTES

TWO

GETTING READY TO HEAL

You gain strength, courage, and confidence by every experience in which you really stop to look fear in the face....You must do the thing you cannot do.

Eleanor Roosevelt

The most important part of healing is to tell your story. To do that you need knowledge and information about rape. You must learn the facts about rape for two reasons: First, your personal power was taken from you. Since knowledge is power, learning the facts about rape will help restore some of your lost power. Secondly, nearly everybody has opinions about rape, but few have accurate facts. Having the knowlege will help you separate fact from fiction, and assist in your healing. You won't have to take time to entertain faulty opinions or myths.

The Facts

Rape is an all-American crime. It is the ultimate merging of sex and violence. It is the only crime where the survivor is an "alleged" victim. For example, no one questions your victim status when there is a robbery, when something is stolen from you. But it is not so with rape. This comes out of the societal belief that women are responsible for men's behavior and that men cannot control themselves. It comes from the belief that rape is motivated by sexual urges. Our society believes that women provoke rape, ask for it, and therefore deserve it. The attitude often expressed is that it wasn't his fault. Yet, survivors know that they never asked to be terrorized, or to give up control of their bodies willingly. Myths die hard.

Another popular myth is that women fantasize about being raped. In a fantasy, you are in control and the primary feeling is pleasure. You can start or stop the sexual fantasy of being "taken" whenever you desire. However, the reality of rape is quite different--you are stripped of any control or personal power. The overriding, primary emotion is terror--not pleasure.

Rape itself may be a form of murder. It destroys one's will and spirit. It robs you of your self-respect. It strips you of your privacy and leaves you in a state of fear and anxiety that can last for weeks, sometimes months, sometimes years. It is the physical mastery of the stronger over the weaker.

A feminist hypothesis about rape is that it is inherent in relationships between men and women. Rape is one way to continue the domination of women and children. One man's rape contributes to the power of all other men in society. This idea received considerable attention in Susan Brownmiller's book *Against Our Will* which was published in 1975.

In 1982 an anthropologist from the University of Pennsylvania compared data from many cultures to find that rape was anything but universal. Dr. Sunday found patterns of behavior common to what she calls "rape prone" societies. These "rape prone" societies are very different from traits of "rape free" peoples. Societies with high incidences of rape, such as the United States, tolerate violence and encourage men and boys to be tough, aggressive and competitive.

Conversely, we encourage women to be passive and submit to force or the threat of force.

Men in the so-called "rape prone" cultures generally have special, politically important gathering spots that are off limits to women, such as men's clubs or neighborhood pubs. Women have little or no part in public decision making or religious rituals. Men scorn women's practical judgement, demean what they consider women's work, and remain distant in child bearing or child rearing.

Dr. Sunday found that in "rape free" cultures women are generally respected. They are influential members in the community. They are generally recognized for their unique contributions to the general well being of the community and are prominent in religious life.

In biblical times sex was sanctioned between men and young girls. It was an acceptable means of betrothal and the use of both girls and women was regulated by a detailed set of laws regulating the property status of females. Women and girls were owned, rented and sold as sexual commodities. As long as these transactions were conducted with proper payment by the males, rabbis and lawmakers approved.

The sexual use of girls under three was not regulated legally because they were too young to be considered legal virgins and were, therefore, without monetary value. So sex with a child under the age of three was not subjected to any regulation. Boys under the age of nine were also fair game. For these children, it was always open season.

The advent of Christianity did not change things much. Cannon law established that sexual intercourse meant possession and Popes throughout the centuries upheld rape as an indissolvable means of contracting marriage. Christian law did raise the age of legally valid sex from three to seven and sexual intercourse with girls over seven became legally binding. Sexual intercourse with girls under seven was again of no consequence to the authorities because their virgin status held no monetary value.

Rape as spoils of war is cross-cultural. Cossacks raped Jewish women and children, Pakistanis raped Bengali women and children, Americans raped Vietnamese women and children, Germans raped French women and children.[1]

As you can see from the above, rape as a right of passage, rape as a reward of war, rape as a right of the stronger over the weaker has a long historical base. It is deeply imbedded in our history and in our culture. You were a victim of a barbaric, primitive practice that is still alive and well in the 20th century.

Several good books that may help you understand rape are listed in the back of this book. Perhaps you'll want to read more about the history and dynamics of rape. The following section looks at what we know about rapists in general.

Characteristics of a Rapist

As previously indicated, rape is a complex crime with a long history and is not easily understood. It is also the reason that your reactions to your victimization are hard to understand. So, too, are rapists. While rapists can't be put into nice, neat categories, enough is known about them to draw some general conclusions. They are angry people, but some are masters at hiding their anger. Often, one hears "He's the nicest person you'll ever meet," or "Not him—he'd never do anything like that!"

A rapist can be anyone. Rapists can be professional men with power. They can be men of high position, good standing in their church and in their community. They may be strangers. But more often they are people known and trusted. Although rare, rapists can be women. The popular myth is that they are dirty old men or sex-starved maniacs who are driven by passion with no self-control. Popular opinion also holds that sex offenders generally do not repeat their crime. Actually unless stopped, they rape over and over in a cycle that is unbroken. Let's examine what rapists believe about themselves and their victims. What motivates them?

The fact is, male rapists both hate and fear women. They are incapable of having equal relationships with women. Generally, they have unequal relationships with everyone in their lives. They overtly or subtly discount others or put them down. They may appear self-confident, personable, likeable and have lots of friends. But, if you look closely, you'll find that they have no real close or intimate relationships.

Rapists do not like themselves very much. They chose the crime of rape as a way to satisfy their need to dominate. For these people, the only way to have personal power is to take it. They are empty inside and feel that control is external, outside of them. They have the idea that the only way to get personal power is by taking it from women. You can begin to understand why it is the rare offender who rapes only once. After all, how long can the feelings of dominance, power and control last once the crime has been committed? In order to recapture these powerful feelings, he will rape again.

Their idea of dominance is acted out in their crimes depending on what kind of person they have become. Some survivors describe their offenders as Dr. Jekyll and Mr. Hyde. "Suddenly, he changed. Something snapped. The look in his eyes changed and there was absolutely no warning." Others say the rapist was inhuman from the start. Stories of brutality unleashed are not uncommon. Those are the ones generally read about in the news media. The vast majority of rapes never make the news. This may be one reason that some think that unless you are physically brutalized and threatened with a weapon, it was not rape.

Beliefs and Attitudes

Rapists hold the belief that real men can do anything they want with women. They believe that "no" means "yes" and that if they are persistent enough they will succeed in getting what they want. Women are supposed to say "no" even when they mean "yes," otherwise they might be considered "easy." They also believe that women are supposed to be submissive and passive, so they overcome a woman's willingness to resist with their persistence. There comes a point when it is wiser to submit than to resist because of the fear of what will happen if you don't. It's not that victims can't resist in most cases, it is that they are afraid to.

Sexual assault happens in a variety of ways. Does it surprise you to know that most rapes are planned? For example, he may have you out for an evening and what he expected in return for his money was sex. When sex is refused he feels provoked. When you did not live up to your end of the unspoken bargain, sex was forced and that is rape. He will typically feel justified because you provoked him by accepting his favors.

When rapists feel provoked (and their definition is the only one that counts) they believe you have no right to deny them sex. They think that there is a point of no return and when that point is reached they cannot be denied sex. Remember, provocation can mean anything the rapist wants it to mean. It's his excuse.

The above beliefs and attitudes are held by many people. You may recognize your own beliefs reflected in some of the above and yet, you were a victim. In part your own values and beliefs may contribute to the guilt and confusion you feel.

Background and Motivations

Rapists come from all walks of life. Some are poor and disadvantaged, while some come from homes of abundance. Most missed true closeness in their families. Many witnessed or experienced physical and emotional abuse or isolation. They were alienated from those who could have or should have provided love and closeness. Some were sexually abused. Because they feel life for them was filled with personal rejection, they cannot handle rejection in any form as adults. When they perceive rejection from their victims, they feel rage and anger emerge. The act of rape then becomes a reflection of their personal inadequacy acted out. It is important to remember that the rapist had a choice—you didn't.

As one rapist put it, "I wanted to put the anger I felt in someone else's body. The anger wouldn't go away with just hitting things. It had to be in another person's body. I 'got off' making her do what I wanted." Sexual assault is the way this rapist expressed his own anger and bitter feelings.

At the end of the rape, often the offender feels relief from both the anger and anxiety that lead up to the rape. Most importantly, he feels justified. His self-worth is restored because he has been able to dominate another person and he feels powerful again. Once again, the myth that you caused the rape shatters in the face of understanding.

Rape happens half the time in victims' homes or in the homes of the rapists. It happens every hour of the day and night. It happens 60-70% of the time by someone the survivor knows. Most rape is by men who won't take "no" for an answer. Most rape is done by men who just won't stop.

Who Can You Tell?

For some survivors there seems to be no one they can trust to tell about the rape. You may feel isolated and ashamed of what happened and feel you can never tell anyone about this experience. You think friends, partners, parents or authorities will not believe you. They may blame you. You feel it was your fault, or it was so long ago that you think people will find you foolish for allowing it to still be a factor in your life. Perhaps you found a new relationship and you think your new partner will reject you or find you undesirable, soiled or dirty, if he finds out. Furthermore, what if the person who raped you is your very own husband, lover or partner, and if you bring it up, he will do it again! Maybe the rapist is your boss or someone with whom you go to school. Who will believe you? After all, you think, it's your word against your rapist's.

There seems to be no place to go, no one to tell for all the reasons listed above and yet, your life continues to deteriorate. It's like you are on a downhill slide and once again helpless to stop the destruction of your life. You reach a point where you can no longer live with the secret and must take the risk of telling someone. You must reach out and trust someone despite the risks.

Who can you tell, and where can you get the support you so desperately need?

Rape Crisis Centers

There are several options. The best is to get in touch with a rape crisis center. The big fear you have—that no one will believe you—will come to an end. Rape crisis centers are places where people believe survivors. They exist to support, to counsel, and to advocate for you. They can help you figure out who is a safe person for you to turn to for the calm, unwavering support you need. Many centers have individual counseling as well as groups that you can attend.

Because rape rarely happens with an audience, many survivors believe that their feelings are unique. They believe that no one else in the world could have feelings like theirs. Yet there is comfort in knowing that others have faced the same awful ordeal and understand your feelings.

Perhaps you feel that everyone can just look at you and tell you are a survivor of rape. One woman, on her first visit to a group said, "Everyone looks so normal." You are normal. Sexual abuse or assault happens to one in three women sometime in their lifetime. Sexual abuse and/or assault happens to one in four girls before their eighteenth birthday and one in six boys. One-fourth of all victims are gang raped. Some estimate that as many as 40 million Americans are suffering from some form of sexual abuse today.

It's healing and comforting to know that you are not alone with the secret. If a rape crisis center is not available to you, then you must concentrate on who you can trust to give the comfort you need as you tell your story. Some counseling centers, mental health professionals, as well as some clergy have received special training to deal with survivors of rape. There will be many decisions to make along the way, and choosing the right people to tell is an important step. The benefits are numerous.

How Will I Benefit From Telling?

As long as you keep a bad secret your life becomes contaminated by that secret. You cannot be completely free with others because you must always be on guard not to let the secret out. You hold back part of yourself and that takes energy that could be used to enhance your relationships. As long as you keep the secret it rolls around in your heart and brain, bouncing off the surfaces or seeping into crevices and never sees the light of day. Without the feedback of others, your worst fears can grow bigger and become distorted.

In the privacy of your mind, you go over it time and time again and it doesn't get any clearer. In fact, it probably gets more cloudy because you haven't found a way to express it. The end result is that you rationalize it. You say that it must have in some way been your fault and so it is a private, personal problem that you need to work out yourself. The fact is that unless you find someway to express what you are thinking and feeling, you stay trapped in the muck created by someone else's criminal behavior.

Making the List

Begin by listing those people in your life that have a need to know. If your school work is suffering or your job is on the line, perhaps the school counselor or your boss need to know. You've already made a list of how this rape has affected your life. Look for areas where telling a trusted person will alleviate some stresses.

Who Needs to Know?

Medical people need to know. There is no way that you were responsible for what happened to you. However, you are responsible for the healing, because as unfair as it is, you alone can heal yourself. You need protection from diseases and pregnancy. The police can help you keep safe; they can investigate and issue warrants for the rapist's arrest. Calling to report a rape to the police must be your decision. While society might be better served if every survivor reported rape to the police, this is sometimes, and for some people, not a good idea. The decision is completely your own.

Who Do You Want to Know?

There may be a few people that you want to know. They are the people who are always there for you during the good and the bad times. They are the people who love and support you. You will need to create a special network of people you can talk with as you begin to tell your story. If possible, choose several on this list because as you begin the active part of the healing, you will need support at different times and not everyone will be available at all times.

Choosing the Right Time

After you have decided who needs to know and who you want to know, the next step is deciding when and how to tell them. You will need to choose a time when neither you nor they will be distracted. Don't set yourself up to be rejected now that you've come so far. For example, telling your father or mother as they leave for work when they have no time to comfort you will not let you receive what you need. Telling your partner when you both are tired may set you up for rejection because there is little energy to spare. Most of us need to hear that the listener believes us. Ask to hear those comforting words.

Just as rape left you in shock, you might expect those you tell to have some of the same reactions you had. They may exhibit anger, disbelief that such a terrible tragedy could have happened to someone they care about, or extreme sadness. They may want to know why you waited so long to tell them. Allow for these feelings and stay with it. While none of us can completely predict how another will react to the news, most will move quickly through their own trauma over the rape and be there to support and care for you.

STEPS TO TAKE

Before you continue on, make a list of those people:

- Who you can tell.
- Who needs to know.
- Who you want to know.
- Decide on the right time to tell them.

As soon as you are ready, move on to the next phase. You've gained some power and control already and you've put your support system in place. What must be done next is to tell the story so that those awful, painful events can be purged from your heart and mind, and the freedom that comes with self-disclosure can be yours.

NOTES

THREE

FEELING THE PAIN

. . . Blunt the sharpness,
Untangle the knot,
Soften the glare. . .

Lao Tsu

Telling the story of what happened to you can be done in many ways. You may choose to see a counselor at a rape crisis center or attend a group of survivors. You may choose a friend or relative to hear you as you begin to share the pain of the rape. Perhaps you cannot identify anyone right now that you want to hear your painful experience. If that is the case, then you can put the pain into words on paper by writing the story. Any of these ways will be helpful and healing. The point is to express it.

Every rape holds meaning. You may interpret the event to mean, for example, that you are no longer desirable in a sexual way, that you are dirty or unworthy. Maybe you tell yourself that you are incapable of making good decisions, or that your independent lifestyle must come to an end because you are too vulnerable, too old, too unsafe to be left alone. Look for themes and meaning that come up as you tell your story because it will give you insight into yourself. That insight becomes more important as you embrace the task of rebuilding.

In the process of telling your story, you will probably re-experience some of the same feelings you had during the rape. It's scary. It's hard and it takes courage to do it. But you can begin now to establish a safety net.

Fear

What triggers the fear? Does it seem to be present all the time? Are there special situations or places where it becomes apparent? Now that the actual event has passed and is part of your history, it is safe to look at the fear. In the telling of the story of your rape, the fear that you felt will return. There are several ways to deal with it. First, you can perform a reality test. That means checking out what frightens you. If you hear noises in the house or work place that alarm you, investigate the noise to reassure yourself that you are safe.

It is important to feel as safe as possible during this period. It is okay to check the door several times to make sure it's locked. It is okay to turn on all the lights at night, to look in every closet and under every bed. Since one of the results of rape is that you believe your ability to make good decisions has been compromised, and that you can't trust your own judgement, it's okay to be compulsive about safety.

Identify the Fears

The second thing to do is to make a list of what frightens you. On the back of the list, make a corresponding list of what to do when you feel that particular fear. For example, if the ringing of the doorbell or a rap on the back door produces fear, then you might want to call a neighbor or friend on the phone and ask them to hold on while you answer the door. Make sure you set that up ahead of time. That way you won't feel so alone or vulnerable. I remember working with a nurse whose fear kept her from sleeping soundly. When we began to talk about what happened when she awoke, she immediately looked at the bedroom door. Changing sides of the bed with her husband, placing him between her and the door produced a sense of safety and protection for her.

To restore your sense of trust in your judgement, you may need to check the door twenty times to assure yourself that it is locked. The reason to make a list of what frightens you and the corresponding list of what to do, is that during the fearful time, it is unfair to expect yourself to solve the problem while involved in it. If you know what to do before you experience the fear, you are more willing to let it happen.

Conventional wisdom recommends that you face the thing that frightens you. Some people while attempting to do that put themselves in dangerous situations physically and psychologically. One woman who was raped in a park, in an act of defiance, went back to that park alone at midnight. The things she hoped to accomplish were to conquer her fear and to make a bold statement that she would not be intimidated again. Both her goals were important but there are smarter and safer ways to accomplish those goals. So, in choosing what you can do to feel safe in a particular situation, be smart. Don't create a further risk for yourself.

Flashbacks and Nightmares

As you begin to relive the rape, flashbacks and nightmares are likely to appear. It is a sign of unearthing the trauma and it is temporary. Some survivors have described a flashback as a movie that starts playing in front of their eyes. Scenes from the rape come back at unexpected, unpredictable times. There is no way to stop the flashbacks from happening. However, you can control the impact they have on your life.

While you are re-experiencing the rape in some form, you can ground yourself in the here and now. That is, you can tell yourself that you are safe, and prove it by touching something concrete. You should name the date and time and reassure yourself that the rape is not happening now. While there may be times throughout your life that something triggers a remembrance, or flashback, they will subside in intensity and frequency as you work through the trauma of the assault. Practice grounding yourself in time and space so that the impact will be less frightening.

There is a way that you can get a sense of retribution through your very own nightmares! Often dreams are a way you are trying to work out something in your life. Old scenes are being replayed, both pleasant and not so pleasant events. For survivors, the nightmares sometimes continue night after night with the same terror, but you can do something about that. Just as you can control the fear brought on by flashbacks by grounding yourself in the here and now, you can take control of the end of the dream.

First, talk or write out the dream. Next, decide how you would like to see the dream end and invent a new dream with the ending you like. Before you go to sleep each night, think about the dream and how you want it to end. It may take several nights of "reprogramming" until you dream the ending that you have created. It can and will work. Once again, you will regain control in an area in which you felt powerless. You no longer need to be afraid to go to sleep because the reoccurring dreams will no longer hold fear for you.

Depression

When you can safely allow yourself to relive the trauma of rape, fear and anxiety seem to slip away out of focus. The nature of fear keeps you revved-up, hypervigilant. When it begins to subside, you may feel depressed. Throughout the experience of rape, your emotions are extreme. In this case you are either on guard with all senses operating at full capacity or flat, dull, gray, deep in depression. The range of emotion swings on a wide spectrum. The goal is to get back a balance in your life. The way to get there is to experience the extremes.

All of your emotions work for you and depression is no different. It slows you down, it gives you time to think. Use the time to delve into depression to see what messages are there for you. Perhaps you can identify with the feelings expressed below:

I'm so tired. Even after many long hours of sleep, I'm so tired. I dread morning. It means going through another gray, cloudy day even though the sun may be shining brightly. All my days and nights are a struggle. Interacting, talking and even listening to others is a struggle.

It began to happen like this for me shortly after the rape. What I mean is that life itself lost its light and I have become a person who only sees the gray and black. I no longer notice if there are reds, yellows, or blues in the world. I used to love the morning, but now I curse the light. It signals the beginning of consciousness. Why can't I sleep until this nightmare ends? What cruel force beckons me to walk through another day like a zombie, a half-dead person? And, when I stop to take note of it as I am now, bitterness fills me up. I can even taste the vileness in me that has replaced the sweetness.

What are the unique messages in your depression? Survivors of rape find issues of guilt, "why me?" shame, embarrassment and stupidity make up most of the depression. The questions recur:

Do I feel guilty because I believe that I asked for it? Could I have resisted more? Did he rape me because I gave him the opportunity?

This may be the time when you can look more objectively at the facts of rape, and what many women are taught to believe about their responsibility for sexual contact.

Guilty feelings about the rape come from a variety of sources. In the creation story, Eve was called first temptress and, therefore, responsible for the downfall of Adam and the loss of innocence. Because women have been cast in that light from the beginning, it follows that they are seen as responsible for men who can't control themselves. Women must have done something to cause the rape, and continue to pay the price. The following news item from Madison, Wisconsin represents the attitude of many Americans toward rape:

Amos Smith was sentenced to 14 years in prison for sexual assault yesterday despite his attorney's argument that violence against women is acceptable in American culture. His attorney, Roger Merry of Belleville, argues that Smith, 30, should not be sent to prison 'for being a victim of culture.' 'Hostility toward women, I think, is something that is culturally instilled in men,' Merry said. 'It's part of our culture that has been for hundreds of years, that violence against women is not unacceptable.' (Seattle Times, September 1, 1982.)

For many centuries society has confused sexual activity and sexual violence. It is believed that any activity in which our sexual organs are involved is sexual activity and distinctions are not made between willing participation and force or coercion. Further, there is the belief that in romantic love, men must dominate, overcome resistance and that men have the right to impose their will regardless of the wishes of women. Confusion for both men and women result from this idea, sometimes leading to violence which is not recognized as rape by men or women.

Another reason for the guilt is that the rapist may have told you that you really wanted him to rape you, that you secretly desired it, and you got what you deserved. That feeling could have been reinforced, especially if your body responded to stimulation. Maybe he chastised you for leaving a window open or a door unlocked. Considering what is known about a rapist's need to dominate and humiliate, can you begin to see how he shifted the responsibility to you? Can you see how he justified and rationalized his own actions by blaming you?

Lastly, guilt comes out of your inability to stop it from happening. "I should have, or I ought to have, or I wish I had..."

A young girl rape victim, 13 years old, asked:

Why did he choose me? There were three of us waiting for our parents to pick us up after the movie. Why did he grab me and not one of my friends?

Do you wonder? Do you believe it was because of something you did or said? Do you believe that it is punishment for some bad behavior in your past of which you are ashamed?

It is natural to look at the rape and search for your own responsibility for it. It is what you've been taught to do in all other areas of your life. The difference here is that the rapist gave you no choice. Begin now to substitute the following questions for those you are asking yourself:

- Do I have the right to refuse to have sex with someone?
- Is someone infringing on my rights when that person forces me to have sex?
- Do I need to feel shame if I really did not have a choice?
- Is it reasonable to feel guilty for being the victim of an attack?

Anger

Rape is the ultimate violation of the self, short of murder. The effects are in some ways unique because of the self-blame. The embarrassment of having it happen combined with the feelings of shame and stupidity give rise to questions as to whether there are basic human rights at all. You must mourn your loss. You must grieve your loss of innocence, maybe your loss of virginity, your independence. The depression gives you time and space to do those tasks and, therefore, it has value. At the end of the depression, when new questions have been asked and answered and the mourning enters a new phase, comes anger.

In the grieving cycle, anger comes before depression. For many survivors, however, expressing anger comes only when it feels safe to do so. Whichever your unique style dictates is normal. The goal is to pass through each phase of healing your way and with as much control as you can have.

Now that you know that the rape wasn't your fault--it was his fault and what he did was to violate your human rights, anger and rage bloom full. It's unrelenting! It colors everything you do. You probably see the world and everyone in it as an enemy as the woman below did:

> *I'm waiting for the slightest hint that someone has wronged me or is likely to. I blast the grocery clerk because she overcharges me by ten cents. I curse the driver ahead of me for being indecisive. The people who serve me, the waiters, the taxi drivers, the sales-people all have felt my outbursts and they don't deserve it. It was not meant for them.*

Like other emotions, you have to first experience anger before you can label it. The woman quoted above is beginning to recognize how she is reacting to her anger and beginning to know that a form and direction are trying to emerge. No memories are ever truly buried, they only go into cold storage. All of them must be examined and worked through otherwise they show up uncontrollably in thoughts and feelings. The result is that you often think you are "crazy," when what is happening is that it is time to know the anger.

Anger as a reaction to rape is the most appropriate feeling you have and it is a sign of emerging strength. The task is to manage it and at the same time, give it full expression. As depression served to slow you down so that you could think, anger serves as a guide to be clear about decisions you want to make about your rapist. So, welcome to this powerful, sometimes frightening, often rewarding feeling!

Just as safety was an important part of feeling the fear, safety is important while experiencing anger. There are different ways to express it. So give it full voice without abusing either yourself or others. But first, consider the prohibitions against the natural expression of women's anger.

You were probably taught that anger was unacceptable. Women who express it are called "uppity bitches," unfeminine, hysterical, out of control, or castrators, to name a few. When you express anger, it goes against the injunctions to please others first. It flies in the face of your role as peace maker, nurturer, and soother. Unlike men who are applauded and affirmed for the expression of anger, women are condemned. They are said to be unloving and unlovable.

Anger handled wisely produces change. That is why people are afraid of it. The resolution of anger means challenge, change, and becoming someone different.

While you may be unhappy with who you are right now, at least there is comfort in the known and familiar. You avoid anger because you feel that if you express it, if you really let go, the intensity of the anger will kill anyone close to you. Your anger will crack the world! If you give it full reign, then you will be lost forever to insanity. Many believe that having a feeling or thought is the same thing as doing the thought or feeling. Start now to separate feelings and thoughts from behavior.

Strategies for Dealing With Anger

There are several options for getting in touch with anger and expressing it safely. One way is through fantasy. Whatever way you have chosen to tell your story to a friend, a counselor, a group of other survivors, or through your writing, use the gift of fantasy. Feel free to imagine just what you would like to see happen to your rapist. Talk it through, embellish it, savor it, create the perfect punishment. Use all your senses in this exercise. What does the punishment look like, sound like, feel like? Does the punishment have a color, a taste or a smell? You will have your own unique ideas about the perfect revenge for what was done to you.

There is no need for concern because the safety net is in place. This is **your** perfect world, created by **you,** and **you** are in complete control. This is a creative process, it is meant to give you a sense of justice—not to be acted out. For if it were acted out, it would be difficult to separate yourself from the criminal who took away your right to control your own body. And, no survivor wants to identify in any way with the person who raped her.

Sometime, survivors say:

'I know I should feel angry and intellectually I do, but I can't seem to get to it emotionally,' or 'But I love him. How can I be angry with him and still love him?'

If that is where you are, collect some art supplies. Draw, color, use clay to create what you think anger looks like. Notice what colors you have chosen.

Have you chosen pastels? Have you drawn a blue sky with white puffy clouds? You probably used bright, hot colors. How often did you use the color black? Are your lines nice and neat or are there black, red or purple marks scrawled on the page? How big is the paper you've chosen? Small pieces of paper probably will not suffice. Have you collected paper as big as newspaper print? Anger takes a lot of room!

What did you build with the clay and what did you do with it after you created it? Once during a group meeting of survivors, four women built penises. They laughed nervously, felt some embarrassment, and on an unspoken cue, they smashed them with their clinched fists. Anger was released.

Movement is another way to release anger. Some survivors receive relief through dance and exercise. In addition to the release of anger, there are numerous benefits to fresh air and exercise. Do what you can physically to increase your level of energy. You will need it as you move into the phase of making new decisions for your life.

When you acknowledge the anger by leaning into it, other issues are unearthed that you are angry about. Anger is a natural emotion but because many women have never been encouraged to express it, or been taught constructive ways to handle it, you may open Pandora's Box. You can feel overwhelmed when you realize the depth of it.

Your first inclination may be to attack on all fronts at once! Be careful with yourself. It would be easy to turn your righteous anger loose and become distracted from the task at hand. Constructive anger must be directed and your task is to decide how you want to deal with the rapist.

Some survivors don't have the choice of seeing their attacker brought to justice. For those who do, the legal system can serve as a vehicle to carry the anger. At the trial of one rapist who was responsible for 30 known attacks on women, the survivor heard the guilty verdict with a sentence of 99 years. She cried with joy, felt relief, vindicated, believed and incredibly powerful. While nothing can take away the rape, you can and will recover. You are a survivor after all!

STEPS TO TAKE:

- Make a list of your fears.
- After each fear, write down how you are going to handle it.
- Give expression to your anger by working with clay, drawing pictures of it, writing about it, etc.
- List your reasons for and against reporting/bringing charges against the rapist.

When you feel ready to begin anew, and make decisions, move ahead to the next chapter. Stay with any part of the process as long as you need to or want to. The healing is in your hands. No one can do it for you and no one knows exactly how you feel. You have made a commitment to heal--that's why you're reading this book. Let your commitment be your focus.

FOUR

NEW DECISIONS

Freedom has always been an expensive thing.

Martin Luther King

Do you feel like parts of you are unfamiliar? Is it like having someone foreign living in your body? Do you feel like you have changed in some essential way and there is not an ease with those changes yet? Some survivors discover new parts of themselves as a result of rape. They discover, for example, that they have given up too much, have adapted too well to the world and its expectations. Too often, women find that they have put their own needs and desires last and followed someone else's script.

Are you surprised to find your own strength and courage? In the midst of this trauma, there is room now for some admiration of the fact that you used your head. Whether or not you resisted passively or aggressively, you survived, and that took strength and courage. Before moving on to other steps in this ongoing process of healing, look at the way you were before the rape. It's time to say goodbye to those parts that are gone, perhaps forever, and begin to see what has taken their place. It's time to spend some time and energy on you—not the rapist—not your friends or family—just you.

Before the rape you probably had a kind of innocence about people. We all live with faith that others really won't hurt us, that crimes like rape happen to other people. You may have believed that you could never be a target, a victim of such an assault. That faith was shaken and the result may be that the fear has generalized. Perhaps your rapist was a person of another race, or a man with blue eyes and blond hair, or maybe you are unable to identify him as black, white, middle eastern, or latin.

A result can be that you are unable to distinguish between who is a threat and who isn't. Maybe you become anxious in the presence of all blond, blue-eyed men. A part of you knows that this reaction is unreasonable, but the part of you that remains fearful won't allow you to take the smallest risk. The questions become, "Who am I? What part of me can I trust? Can I trust myself at all?" Conflict between the old and the new battle for your allegiance while you remain confused over what was and what is.

In this fast-paced world, confusion is a luxury. People expect that you will make decisions and move forward. Mourning the loss of innocence takes time, and confusion is often a companion to grieving.

Safety

Part of the experience of rape raises questions of dependence and independence. This is the point where you begin to assert yourself in a new way. Take the time you need to be with the pain of the loss of innocence. There are people who will hurt, take from you, and try to destroy your will and spirit and you know it. There are many more who will respect your right to your own body, who will support and protect you. Spend time with people who support your healing process.

Probably you are a person who believed that you could take good care of yourself and were proud of your independent lifestyle. Now, you think that was stupid and feel embarrassed. You think you must have been arrogant in being proud. Yet, with the courage it takes to heal, you know that you have strength and determination.

It makes sense to live in a more protected environment just now because it takes, in addition to courage, energy to heal. When you feel more in balance, the independence that was yours and that you were rightfully proud of will return. In the meantime questions remain about independence and dependence causing distortions. Be with them. Let them exist and give them expression. It is not possible to attend to all issues at once, nor is it respectful to the healing self. It takes time as well as patience.

Sexuality

In addition to having been raped, the memory of the rape robs you of your most intimate way of sharing yourself after the assault. This can be one of the hardest parts of the rape for many survivors because sex before the rape was an experience entered into with pleasure and as an equal. Now you may feel blocked, cut off from that very private and personal way of sharing yourself.

In your struggle to understand, you are likely to label incorrectly the reason for the lack of desire. You may say that you're somehow incomplete or damaged or dirty or undeserving of sexual pleasure. Most women have received and accepted societal messages that they are totally responsible for their sexual organs. If that is true and you believe it, then you are somehow at fault because you failed in your duty to protect yourself. Therefore, that which is uniquely you, that which was yours to give and share, that which was so special, is gone. And you grieve.

The reality is that the traumatic memories of the rape are anchored in your sexuality. Even a welcome touch can bring forth the memory of the rape and you may be unable to control your reaction because you couldn't control the attack. Because of the unique nature of rape, the invasion of your body, giving yourself over to someone you care about can be full of fear and anxiety. The fact is that with some time, the desire returns as the healing deepens. What is needed is nurturing and acceptance that your body, as well as your heart and mind, needs time to heal. Give yourself that time. Once again, faith in yourself, patience with yourself is what is necessary for the sexual desire to return.

The trauma of rape set you back for a time. The opportunity here is to examine what you want to change, what you want to be different, and when the time is right, to take some action to make your life the way you want it to be.

Any crisis brings into focus problems and conflicts that were present before. When you survive any crisis, the problems and conflicts that were in your life take on new meanings. Either you see them for what they really are about or they become much deeper and more serious.

Handling the Reactions of Others

The people in your life whom you tell about the rape can have a variety of responses. The crisis of rape can be threatening to the men in your life. Men are socialized to be the protectors of the family and even though the rape may have happened when he was not with you, he may believe that he failed in his protective role. This response can be the same for fathers, brothers, husbands, lovers, or boyfriends.

The reaction may be one of great anger toward the rapist. He may want to kill the person who did this to you. It is hard for anyone to nurture while angry. Since the rapist may be unknown or never caught, your partner's anger may be directed toward you. He may want to know why you were out alone. One woman was on her way to work when she had a flat tire. As she walked toward a service station, she was raped. Her husband wanted to know why she had left her car. Most of us, including him, would have tried to get help for a flat tire. Her problem solving ability was sound. However, because her rapist was never caught, her husband needed an outlet for his anger. He had "failed" to protect her and when he could not find the appropriate outlet for his anger, she became the target.

42

There is a belief in our society that if you have an auto accident, you should drive again as soon as possible so that you won't be frightened of driving. The sooner you do this, the less chance there will be for you to become too traumatized to drive. If you fall off a horse, then you should get right back on the horse to overcome your fear.

Some lovers believe this analogy applies to rape situations as well. They demand that you have sex again soon after the rape. They reason that sex is what you are frightened of, then the most therapeutic thing you can do for yourself is have sex again as soon as possible.

What men sometimes fail to realize is that sex was the weapon used to accomplish the assault. Most survivors are responding to the assault, to the threats that were used to accomplish the rape. Your heart and mind remember and so does your body. Therefore, the demand for sex as soon as possible can only traumatize you further and has no therapeutic value. You lost control of your body during the assault and you must be allowed to take it back at your own pace. You must be the one to initiate sexual activity when your body has had a chance to heal from the memory of the assault.

For some men, the demand for sex is a way to assert their right over the right of the rapist. It is a way to once again lay claim to what they see as theirs. Most of the time, the intentions of the men in our lives are honorable. They may truly believe that if you fall off a horse, then the best medicine is to get back on immediately. They may truly believe that they must reassert their right to our bodies for "our own good". But these good intentions hurt an already wounded spirit.

Sometimes the reaction is one of distance from you. Some men believe that if another man has sex with his wife or lover, then she is "damaged goods." He believes that she is "soiled" or "dirty" and his ego will not allow him to be where another man has been. So, he withdraws, and it hurts.

Sometimes your losses include some of your women friends as well. Some may withdraw from you in the aftermath of rape. They feel too vulnerable. They think that if it could happen to you, then it could happen to them, and being with you becomes frightening. If they, too, have suffered a rape and their pain is still with them, they may be blocked from giving you the support you need. Your rape recreates their own crisis.

Another response coming out of their fear is to make you different from them. The reasoning goes like this:

I would not have put myself in that position. I wouldn't have left a window or a door unlocked or been out by myself or I would have fought to the death before I'd have allowed myself to be raped. Therefore, because I would have done things differently, not like her, I cannot be raped.

This kind of invalid, untruthful reasoning makes her feel safer. Being with you is a reminder of her vulnerability and so, she withdraws, and it hurts.

It's important to understand that the reactions of your significant others are coming out of their own fears, anger, vulnerability and experiences. It has little to do with you. It has everything to do with what this rape has triggered in their own psyches.

New Insights

Rape changes life. Things will never be the same again. Rape is not an event that you can deny, get behind you or forget. It is an event that must be integrated into your experience just as other major life events have been integrated. With the work you have been doing, integration and healing are taking place. Talking repeatedly about the experience externalizes it. Each time you tell your story, you work out another troublesome aspect and you gain more insight. So long as you keep it inside, the pain of the rape remains in your heart, mind, and body. Once you find a way to talk about it, write about it, draw about it, or whatever other medium you've chosen, the pain becomes externalized and, therefore, much easier to deal with. You gain a perspective that is impossible when the rape remains your secret.

Other things change as well. As the healing intensifies, you become more aware that your self-perception has begun to change. Perhaps you can now see that you are strong and courageous whereas before you might have felt that it was arrogant to acknowledge your strengths. You have probably become more aware—developed greater insight, and have a new criterion for choosing friends. Maybe you had few close friends, but as a result of this experience have broadened your support network. Perhaps you had many acquaintances, but now have a few close friends.

You may resent having to restrict your way of living, while at the same time, it seems prudent to do so. You may not visit the laundry mat at midnight anymore out of a sense of caution. Life may have changed due to the need for more planning and forethought. Maybe you feel cheated because you lack the spontaneity you once had, and mourn the loss of the more naive ways of living. The new lifestyle is like having new shoes. While they aren't well worn or comfortable, they are new and shiny, and there is pride in having them. They make a new statement about you. You feel new, more confident, more determined, more aware and more political. Rape has brought a new awareness of the status of women, men and child victims.

What To Do About The Rapist

When you are ready, you will make some decisions about what kind of relationship or retribution you want for your offender.

Each person has their own style of problem solving. You have been making decisions in some form all your life. You made a decision to survive and you solved the problem of how to do that during the assault. Perhaps you want to look back at that process and the steps it took to solve the problem. Therein lies the answer to how you solve problems, at least under stress.

What do I want to see happen to the person who raped me? Do I want to see that person put on trial and convicted? Do I want to see that person held accountable for his actions publicly or privately? Do I want to confront my attacker in person with others around me? Do I want to confront him privately? In the case where no one is charged and the identity of the attacker is unknown, what options are there for you? Do you want to prosecute?

In any of the above dilemmas, you need to first set a goal before you decide on alternatives or options available to you. Suppose you choose to go to trial. The goal of the prosecutor is to get a conviction and see the rapist punished. Getting a conviction depends on the evidence, how well the prosecution presents the case, and whether the jury believes the state's case. While you support the goals of prosecution, your goal must not depend on conviction, because it is out of your control.

The first thing to know is that from arrest to conviction (in most states) it will take approximately one to three years. On the face of it, having your life put on hold for that long seems like a negative. However, many survivors decide it is worth it. The second thing to know is that the case belongs to the state—not the survivor. The survivor is a witness in the case against the offender. Therefore, the state can, and sometimes does, decide what to do with the case without consulting the survivor.

If the offender pleads guilty, he could receive prison time or probation. The judge, state and defense attorneys could decide on a plea bargain which sometimes reduces the charge if there is a lack of evidence to get a conviction, unavailable witnesses, or it is the first offense for the rapist. Most states out of courtesy, consult with the survivor. However, it is not a requirement.

If the offender goes to trial, you must go on the stand and tell your story. You will be asked many questions about the assault itself, you will be asked to describe how it happened, what he said, what you said, what he did, what you did. A defense attorney will then question you. It is the defense attorney's job to create doubt in the mind of the jurors about your account of the events.

Even in the light of the years it can take, the trauma of having to tell the story of the assault to a courtroom, and the cross examination by the defense, many survivors decide, if given the chance, it is the best decision for them. If you have the option of trial, then the above will need to be considered in your decision-making process. Remember that your wishes are the most important—not the prosecutor's, the rape crisis worker's, your family's, or friend's. It is you who will need to decide if the trial is important to you because it is you who will have to be in touch with the lawyers and the police and the court officials. In addition, you must be willing to deal with the possibility that the rapist may be found innocent. A verdict of innocence does not mean that the rape did not happen, it means that the state simply could not prove it.

If you decide you want to prosecute, the goal of conviction and punishment might not be met. Perhaps you want to consider telling your story in a public forum. Many times that is what the survivors want to do. They need to be heard. Whether or not the jury convicts is not as important as telling their side of the story.

Pressing Charges Against a Friend

Most of the time rape is committed by someone known to the victim. There are many reasons why survivors don't want to go public with the crime. Maybe it was someone whom you love and care about like your partner or husband. What you want is for it never to happen again, and for the rapist to be aware of what he did, and to be sorry. Perhaps what you want is to let him know how this affected your life and to be asked to forgive him. Also you might want a promise, a contract of sorts, that it will never happen again. The goal must be limited to your being able to tell him what you think and how you feel—in other words confrontation. To make the goal dependent on his acknowledging the crime and being sorry for it, places the outcome in the offender's hands, not yours.

What you will need to decide is how to set it up. Who do you want with you or do you want to meet privately? While you may need privacy, remember that abuse thrives in secrecy. Think about how you want to accomplish your goal of confronting your attacker. It is possible that the one you care about doesn't think it was rape. He doesn't accept responsibility for his bad behavior.

The Rapist Hasn't Been Found

In many cases the rapist is never found. The survivors are left wondering whether or not he will find them again and whether or not they will ever be safe from him. What are the options open to the survivors then?

The most important thing is for you to feel complete with the process. The possibilities of his returning to harm you again are indeed remote. But there are steps you can take to insure your safety. If the rape occurred in your home, moving is a consideration. If that is undesirable or not possible, then securing your home with the use of locks and lights is advisable. Secondly, you can use the gift of fantasy as you did in dealing with your anger to imagine what it would be like to be in a court room.

Because your rapist has not been caught does not mean that it is the end of that possibility. Rapists usually don't stop with one rape and it is possible that he will rape again and you will have an opportunity to testify against him at a later point. In the meantime, it is unfair for your life to go on hold, waiting for the capture of the rapist. You deserve better than that. One woman said that the rapist had controlled her life for 12 hours and she would not give him one minute more.

In the midst of any crisis both danger and opportunity are always present. The last section discusses how you can turn this trauma into new life. No one in the world deserves it more than you.

STEPS YOU CAN TAKE

- Identify the changes that have taken place in your lifestyle as a result of the rape.
- Assess what further changes you would like to make:

  For more home security

  To broaden your network or support system
- Review your other list of pros and cons in regard to bringing your rapist to trial. Sort out what you would want to say to him in a confrontation. Plan for it or fantasize it.

NOTES

FIVE

A NEW LIFE -- LETTING GO

We write our own destiny. . .we become what we do.

Madame Chiang Kai-Shek

You've come to the last step in the healing process--letting go. Rape victims must let go and all take this step in their own time. Conversely, no one can tell you when it is your time, but as part of your commitment to healing, it is a necessary step.

Sometimes this is the hardest step to take. To this point attention has been focused on the results of the rape. Now a turning point has been reached and thoughts are concentrated on the present. Full attention will be given to how you are feeling, thinking, and doing now. In the middle of the struggle to understand, feel and be, you know without doubt that you are alive. Pain, as well as joy, has a way of confirming the fact that you can feel life abundantly.

Probably at no time in your life have you focused so completely on yourself. Probably at no time in your life have you had the opportunity to so thoroughly examine your life and what you want out of it. What have you found in that examination? What are the strengths unique to you that you have discovered? Are there some things that you want to change? Have you discovered a new sense of calm and peace? Have you found that paradoxically, you have less need to control?

If letting go means that the intensity in your life will fade, or that your life returns to what it was before, you might be reluctant to take this last step. So let's reason together why it is necessary.

Letting go of the rape means you go on with your life in a healthy manner. Holding on to the pain, the anger and the depression puts limits on your potential growth. Holding on can keep you stuck in a place where you have little or no vision. It can color your insight, sour your soul with bitterness, and keep the barriers to freedom rigid. The rape keeps you prisoner. The rape reaffirms you as a victim. From that point of view, you see the world as a hateful place. Letting go of the pain restores you and enables you to reclaim your personal power.

Rape survivors would not be human if they did not feel hate. But it is an emotion that survivors cannot afford to keep for long. Eventually hate needs healing because it hurts you and it makes you sick.

Survivors attach their feelings to the moment they were raped and give those feelings immortality. Each time they think about the rape, their feelings of hate assault them again. So, letting the hate go, letting the rape take its place in the landscape of your life is self-affirming, self-loving and self-respecting. That is what is necessary throughout the whole healing process and quest for self-respect. Just as you needed to make some decisions about the rapist in order to have your personal power restored, you need to make a decision to let the rape recede into the past.

You are the one to know when it is time to make that decision because after you have walked though the valley of your tears, fears, anger, depression, shame, and guilt, you will be ready. Letting go requires a sense of justice. Consider that living well is the best revenge!

What Letting Go Is Not

Making the decision for a good life does not mean that you must forget what happened. The truth is that you were raped. That is real just like the pain you suffered is real. It profits no one to turn away from the truth. In fact turning away from the truth can make you sick. You will remember what happened, you won't forget, but the memory will not continue to hurt or cause you to feel powerless. Even though you've made a new life, and you've taken this crisis as an opportunity to grow, you will always regret the rape itself. So letting go is not forgetting what happened.

Letting go is not about making excuses for your rapist. It is not about tolerance for this crime. It is not about accepting rape as a part of life. In fact, to excuse the rape is to hold on to the hurt. To excuse fails to accurately place the blame where it belongs--on the offender. To excuse is not to tell the truth. When excuses are made, the tolerance for and acceptance of rape increases which only serves to set one up for the crime again.

How to Let Go

Letting go is a process, a slow process--not an act. You don't just wake up one day and decide that today is the day, although some survivors experience it that way. Some survivors say that one day it just came time to release it. However, upon closer examination, you will probably discover that when the time is right you have been in the process for awhile, especially when you remember the hard work you have accomplished.

Letting go happens slowly. It is a process that rarely goes on any schedule, on anyone's time frame and sometimes feels like it has a life of its own. Just when you think you've done all the work, a memory will present itself that causes you to feel bitter or angry and you feel you have failed in this last step. You have not failed.

Letting go takes practice. Healing takes effort as you well know. It is unreasonable to expect yourself not to have anger and resentment for the painful wrong that was done to you. When you can see that letting go is a process, then you'll understand that having these negative feelings does not signal failure. It may indicate that more work is needed in one area. Consider that your feelings are friendly reminders to look closer.

The self-respect and self-loving steps you have been doing will help you become patient with yourself. Because the trauma of the rape is deep, your emotions can become stuck and you may be feeling them out of habit--not out of material that is current. For example, I once had ulcers. Long after they healed, I would occasionally have painful symptoms. Because I had learned that the pain I felt was a friendly warning I paused to ask myself what I was doing to cause the pain. Did I schedule my activities too tightly, creating too much stress? Was I leaving too little time for self care? Did I eat or drink something that was not good for me? Did I have some unfinished business to clear up with someone? How was I not taking care of myself? When I ran through my list of questions and found no answers, I began to know that my symptoms were "left over" from another time. I then acknowledged the pain and reassured my hurting stomach that all was well and the pain disappeared.

The self respecting person you are becoming demands that you take yourself seriously. That means you must listen to your inner voice. Respect the integrity of your feelings. Your heart and mind are now in partnership with each other and both have an equal voice.

What If It Happens Again!

The voyage of self-discovery has begun, and the quest for respect has been won, renewed for some and the first time for others. Survivors now find a deeper well from which to draw. Most find this awakening within themselves brings new knowledge and wisdom. When your thoughts, feelings and actions are in harmony, the struggle ceases and you will find new, undiscovered personal resources that are more precious than gold. Perhaps it is only now that you can dare to wonder what you would do if it happened again.

You have probably thought about it. Most survivors do. They think about it when trying to understand what happened to them. They think about it when anger and rage emerge. Most make plans to prevent it from happening again. Most say things like, "I'd kill him first!" or "I'd die before I let it happen again." Sometimes they say, "I couldn't endure it a second time," or "I would be a crazy person."

One woman said if it would keep her safe from future attacks, she would put a sign on herself that said, "I've already been raped." From information gleaned, you know that rapists can't be picked out of a crowd and that offenders can be anyone, the terrible possibility exists that rape could happen to you again.

Rape happens in thousands of ways making it difficult to plan for all circumstances. You can help yourself by reducing your risks. You can be more alert and aware of your surroundings. You can listen more closely to your intuitive voice. You can protect yourself by becoming less willing to give your trust so automatically. As survivors have learned, sometimes there are no signs, no warnings, no way to know.

If it happens again, you know two things. First, you can survive and secondly, you can heal. What this experience has taught you is that you have courage, strength, and determination. You are better prepared than you ever thought possible to handle whatever events come your way. You can be satisfied in the knowledge that you have changed in some essential ways, that you are personally powerful and are in control in new ways.

Sonja was 65 years old when I first met her. She had never married and lived in the home where she was born. The rapist entered her house through a window over the air-conditioner. She wept, she mourned her loss in all its stages and she changed. She closed the house and moved to a high rise apartment building. In a matter of months she became the new social director of the building. She planned parties and activities for residents young and old alike. She told me that the rape forced her to make healthier choices about her lifestyle. Sonja thrives in her new life, and so can you.

Where Was Your God?

As your personal boundaries become stronger, more obvious to you, the final step in the healing brings up the question of why and how did your personal God allow this crime to happen to you. Questions like "Why did God let this happen? Why was I not protected? Where was God?" Survivors struggle to understand why they were abandoned, left alone to face this tragedy.

The "Why" questions are inevitable, predictable and the survivor's attempt to understand and regain some control of their lives through getting answers. Because human beings have the unique ability to question, to remember the past and project into the future, you probably want answers to make sense of the rape. You want to find some "good" reason, some "good" cause as to why you were chosen. It is difficult to accept the fact that you were perhaps a random victim.

For survivors who have strong faith in a supreme being some of the answers given to these questions are:

- God was testing my faith;
- God is punishing me for something I've done; or
- God is trying to strengthen my character.

Most survivors search for meaning and purpose because it is painful not to have answers. Most accept the belief that if you do what is right and live in a moral way, then God will protect and reward you. How then can you justify what happened?

Many who have had religious training believe that they should come into God's presence with the faith of a child. Many believe that a strong belief in God means that God will protect them from pain and suffering just as your parents might have. When God does not live up to their expectations, they feel betrayed. They feel both abandoned by and angry with God. Survivors often question if their faith was a fake. Why did they waste their time believing they would be protected because they had a strong faith? Why did they buy into the myth? Why did they allow themselves to be such fools?

What is the opportunity here? Perhaps you can come out of this experience with a more mature relationship with your God. Instead of asking God's protection in your prayers, you might change to asking God to be a partner with you in this world. It is okay to be angry with God.

Just as survivors need to express their anger toward the rapist, they need to express their anger toward God. Just as with other aspects of the rape, they need to rid themselves of the pain so they can be clearer about it. Just as your life will never be exactly the same again, your relationship with God may never be the same again. That is not to say that it will be nonexistent, because as in every crisis there is an opportunity to make life better. An opportunity exists to understand in a new way that what God promises is not life without pain, but a promise of partnership through the suffering and pain.

Perhaps what you will discover is that the purpose is in living more purposefully. That is to say that if you live your life moment by moment, you are able to be more fully alive and engaged in the world.

End of the Quest

You've come to the end of your healing journey. You have grown and changed because you took the first big step. You acknowledged the impact of the rape on your life. You made lists—lots of lists. You made the commitment to the process of healing. You learned that you were not at fault— that you were a victim, not only of the rapist but of a society that encourages and glorifies violence. You learned to face fear and in the middle of it, you learned not to be afraid of fear, depression or anger. You experienced the value of sorrow and learned the power of anger.

You made new decisions about the relationships in your life. You made new commitments about how to be with your new self and affirmed your survivorship. You learned how to be patient with your internal process and most importantly, you learned to respect **your** time frame.

You came away from this experience with a stronger sense of where you are headed and you know the path to reach your goal. Reading this book cannot solve all of your problems relating to the rape, but it can be a guide that has value in your healing and self discovery. It's your life and it always has been. For a time, the rapist took that away from you. You have reclaimed it and you've come out of this stronger, less naive, and more serious. The key to your continuing personal growth is now, as it always has been, a quest for self-respect.

STEPS TO TAKE

- Review the "steps" in previous chapters and add to your lists where indicated.
- Make one last list: Your strengths, old and new, congratulate yourself, and keep it handy for those times when your self-respect falters.
- Reassess your life style and consider if there are any further steps you need to take to avoid re-victimization.
- Reflect on your spiritual goals and decide if there is any action you want to take to redefine them.

NOTES

APPENDIX

END NOTES

1. This information is from, Bass, Ellen, *I Never Told Anyone*, Harper and Row, 1983, New York, N.Y. pp 34-35.

SUGGESTED READING

Bass, Ellen and Thornton, Louise, *I Never Told Anyone*, Harper & Row, New York, NY.

Finklehor, David and Yollo, Kersti, *License To Rape*, Holt, Rinehart & Winston, New York, NY.

Fortune, Marie Marshall, *Sexual Violence: The Unmentionable Sin*,The Pilgrim Press, New York, NY.

Gil, Eliana, *Outgrowing The Pain*, Harper & Row, Walnut Creek, CA.

Johnson, Kathryn, *If You Are Raped*, Learning Publications, Holmes Beach, FL.

Katy, Judy H., *No Fairy Godmother, No Magic Wand: Healing Process After Rape*, R & E Publishers, Saratoga, CA.

Ledray, Linda E., *Recovery From Rape*, Henry Holt & Co., New York,NY.

Lerner, Harriet Goldhor, *The Dance of Anger*, Harper & Row, New York, NY.

Lord, Janice Harris, *No Time For Goodbyes: Coping with Sorrow, Anger, and Injustice After a Tragic Death*, Pathfinder Publishing Co. 458 Dorothy Ave., Ventura, CA.

McEvay, Alan W. and Brookings, Jeff B., *If She Is Raped*, Learning Publications, Holmes Beach, FL.

Neiderbach, Shelly, *Invisible Wounds: Crime Victims Speak*, Halworth Press, New York, NY.

Peck, M. Scott, *People of the Lie*, Simon & Schuster, New York, NY.

Smeder, Lewis, *Forgive and Forget*, Harper & Row, San Francisco, CA.

Viorst, Judith, *Necessary Losses*, Balentine Books, New York, NY.

Warshaw, Robin, *I Never Called It Rape*, Harper & Row, New York, NY.

Williams, Tom, *Post-Traumatic Stress Disorders: A Handbook for Clinicians, Disabled American Veterans*, Cincinnati, OH.

HELPFUL ORGANIZATIONS

Center For Women's Policy Studies
2000 P Street N.W., Suite 508
Washington, DC 20036
(202) 872-1770

Child Help National Child Abuse Hotline
1345 El Centro Ave.
P.O. Box 630
Hollywood, CA 90028
(800) 4A-CHILD

Pennsylvania Coalition Against Rape
2200 North 3rd St.
Harrisburg, PA 17110
(717) 232-6745 (For national directory of rape crisis centers)

National Coalition Against Domestic Violence
1500 Massachusetts Ave., N.W. No. 35
Washington, DC 20005
(202) 347-7017

National Coalition Against Sexual Assault
8787 State St.
East St. Louis, IL 62203
(618) 398-7764

National Criminal Justice Reference Service
Box 6000
Rockville, MD 20850
(800) 851-3420

National Organization for Victim Assistance
717 D St., N.W.
Washington, DC 20004
(202) 393-6682

National Self-Help Clearinghouse
Graduate School
City University of New York
33 W. 42nd St. Room 1222
New York, NY 10036
(212) 840-1259

National Victim Center
307 W. 7th St. No. 1001
Fort Worth, TX 76102
(817) 877-3355

Victims of Incest Can Emerge Survivors (VOICES)
P. O. Box 148309
Chicago, IL 60614
(312) 327-1500

INDEX

ORDER FORM

Pathfinder Publishing of California
458 Dorothy Ave.
Ventura, CA 93003-1723
Telephone (805) 642-9278   FAX (805) 650-3656

Please send me the following books from Pathfinder Publishing:

_____Copies of **Beyond Sympathy** @ $11.95 $____
_____Copies of **I Can't Do What?** @ $14.95 $____
_____Copies of **Injury** @ $9.95 $____
_____Copies of **Living Creatively**
                    With Chronic Illness @ $11.95 $____
_____Copies of **Managing Your Health Care** @ $9.95 $____
_____Copies of **No Time For Goodbyes** @ $11.95 $____
_____Copies of **Quest For Respect** @ $9.95 $____
_____Copies of **Sexual Challenges** @ $11.95 $____
_____Copies of **Surviving an Auto Accident** @ $9.95 $____
_____Copies of **Violence in our Schools, Hospitals and**
                    Public Places   @ $22.95 Hard Cover $____
_____   @ $14.95 Soft Cover $____
_____Copies of **Violence in the Workplace** @ $22.95 Hard $____
             Violence in the Workplace @ $14.95 Soft $____
_____Copies of **When There Are No Words** @ $9.95 $____
                                            Sub-Total $____
              Californians: Please add 7.25% tax. $____
              Shipping* $____
                                            Grand Total $____

I understand that I may return the book for a full refund if not satisfied.
Name:_____

Address:_____
_____ZIP:_____
Credit Card_____ Card No. _____
*SHIPPING CHARGES U.S.
Books: Enclose $3.25 for the first book and .50c for each additional
book. UPS: Truck; $4.50 for first item, .50c for each additional. UPS
2nd Day Air: $10.75 for first item, $1.00 for each additional item.
Master and Visa Credit Cards orders are acceptable.